ACCORDING TO BARCLAY

Reflections On Life in the Human Pack

Dr. Benjamin E. Williams

According to Barclay. Reflections on Life in the Human Pack, by Dr. Benjamin E. Williams.

ISBN: 978-1-304-54064-5

Published by Lulu.com
Printed in the United States of America by Lulu.com.
Distributed by Lulu.com.

In affectionate memory
of
the most excellent Earl Barclay Gray,
curmudgeonly Munch,
and sweet, sweet Maude.

Harret die Morgenroete entgegen.

TABLE OF CONTENTS

PREFACE

A DOG'S LIFE

Yes, Virginia, there is a Barclay...

Barclay – or Earl Barclay Gray - was born July 25, 1997, and was an AKC registered Miniature Schnauzer. I picked him out when he was about two weeks old based on his temperament... and the skeptical way he cut his eyes at me. I asked the breeder to leave the litter intact for at least eight weeks, but he began dispersing the puppies after only four; Barclay was left with a litter of Miniature Pincers for another eight days, then the breeder called me to come pick him up.

So those few key early weeks of his socialization training happened not among dogs, but among people. In spite of that, Barclay turned out to be A Most Excellent Pup.

By the time Ceci and I married, I had two Schnauzers – with a third on the way – and she had three rescue dogs: our "blended family." I became Alpha for a pack of six dogs. I have learned more about group dynamics and leadership from them than I ever did in college and Seminary, and I think I'm a better pastor and crisis manager for it.

In these stories you will meet Barclay and the rest of our pack. There are Barclay's sons: Young Master Braxton Gray, and Lord Benson Cullen Gray. There are my wife's rescue dogs: a mixed-breed Labrador Retriever/Doberman brother and sister, named Munch and Maude, and a tense, somewhat neurotic black-and-tan terrier of debatable ancestry named Gracie. During the course of writing these reflections, we lost

Maude, Munch, and Barclay, all at decrepit old age; their places have been taken now by two female Retrievers rescued from neglectful, abusive situations: Cheyenne and Belle; and a young, abandoned Wire-Haired Dachshund we named Duncan. You won't need to remember their names – I will introduce each dog anew whenever it appears in the book.

Most of the dog stories here are mundane, everyday; a few are extraordinary. All are true. But this is not primarily a collection of dog stories – Barclay was unusual, but his life, as a whole, was not unusual enough to write a whole book about. Rather, this has grown out of a connection, an interface that I have observed between dog and human social behavior. There are a lot of things – both good and bad – humans can learn from dogs. How to live A Dog's Life.

A couple of caveats at the outset: what this book *isn't*. This is not a heart-tugging biography of Barclay, like *Old Yeller* or *Marley and Me*. This is not a manual for pet owners on dog training or psychology, although some of my observations may help you understand your dog(s) a little better. This is not a systematic treatment on either canine or human social interaction. Shoot, the stories aren't even in chronological order. These are merely random reflections, parables, and Christian devotions, each triggered by something I have observed in my little pack.

Some skeptical readers may accuse me of anthropomorphism, that is, of projecting human thoughts and emotions onto my dogs, as if they were little humans. Of course every pet owner is prone to that to some extent, but I know full well: *dogs are not people.* Barclay reminded me of that fact all the time. If I try to treat a dog like a human, it will only confuse and frustrate the dog. Barclay's brain, the dog brain, is built differently than mine, or rather, its functions apportioned differently, to do different things. I do not try to read human thoughts and motivations into his actions: dogs are not self-reflective in the same way humans are. But when a dog does something, he usually does it for a reason that makes perfect sense in *dog* logic. I try to understand that dog logic... because it also can tell us something about unconscious, instinctive *people* logic.

I have read textbooks and talked with trainers who claim dogs don't think or remember or have emotions. I wonder what planet they're on. Research has determined that dogs have the mental capacity of about a four-year-old child – which is actually pretty sophisticated. I have watched a dog knit its brow, deep in thought, trying to figure out how to accomplish some task. This usually has to do with food...but it is still thinking. I have seen Barclay excited over visiting places where he hasn't been in years, or over seeing – or sniffing – people and things that have been gone for months or years. That is memory. I have seen dogs expressing embarrassment, guilt and remorse, grief, concern, sympathy, determination, humor, mischief, loyalty, contentment, joy, gratitude. How many emotions does it take to be emotional? The dismissive treatment accorded dogs by some is, I believe, simply the arrogance of the human species with *just enough* Frontal Lobe to be condescending.

Dogs are above all *social animals*, and they have a highly developed "pack center" in the back of their brain that governs their social relationships. And that is a part of the brain humans share with dogs – I'll touch on that some in these brief essays, and will explain this further in the next book, *Your Inner Dog*. A lot of the unwritten rules of social interaction are similar; this is where we can learn the most. I am not interested in finding the human in dogs, but rather the dog in humans – what I call The Inner Dog.

The Inner Dog drives a surprising amount of human social behavior. It is the seat of ethical decision-making, group loyalty, play. You go to the ball game with your friends: you root for your team and paint your face in team colors (social identification); you get a little choked up with pride in your country as someone stirringly sings the national anthem (loyalty); you jump up and down and scream till it's scary (hunting games); you do NOT kill the umpire or referee (social ethics). All of this behavior is governed by your Inner Dog.

These are thoughts about life, love, society, behavior, the world, and God – all from the perspective of qualities we share with dogs. They are each designed to stand alone, so there is some unavoidable repetition from one to another. I hope you enjoy them, and find them meaningful.

Dr. Benjamin Williams
Reidsville, NC
September 12, 2013

1.

THE SQUIRREL
IN THE ROAD

"Barclay! Car! Stop!" I barked, and I held my breath. Would he?

When I began training my Schnauzer puppy, I didn't want to teach him cute but useless tricks. I wanted to teach him basic life skills, things he would need to know in a world shaped by humans. Things like "Food," "Thirsty," "Hungry," "Walk" he picked up immediately. He learned to roll over by verbal command and by hand signal, so we could hunt fleas. "Come!" – "Go!" – "Up!" – "Down!" – "Over!" – "Through"" became part of his repertoire. At street curb it was "Wait!

...Cross!" and we would look out for "Car!" In his prime, Barclay could recognize and understand over one hundred words and commands. Probably the hardest one to teach him was "Stop!"

In time I could walk Barclay off-leash, guiding him by a series of low whistles and hand gestures. We would walk around the block, checking out the neighborhood scents. Every day or two we'd see a squirrel or rabbit – two words he understood *well.* He would tear off, chasing it up a tree, or into a thicket, and trot back quite pleased with himself.

Barclay *loves* chasing squirrels. Never caught one, even when one doubled-back right between his legs, and as far as I can tell, he's never really *wanted* to catch one. He ran after one once that was lame and ran with a limp, so Barclay *slowed down* so it could get to the tree just a second before he did. True story. It wasn't the catching... it was the *chase.*

Squirrel-chasing was usually fairly safe. There wasn't much traffic on our residential street. The squirrels and rabbits would hightail it to the nearest tree or pole, or thick brush – always *away* from the road. Except once...

The squirrel was hunting nuts at the base of an oak tree up in a neighbor's front yard. Barclay saw it and took off like a rocket. The squirrel saw him, too, and took off... toward a telephone pole between the sidewalk and the road. It waited a moment on the side of the pole and, with Barclay in hot pursuit, leapt into the road and dashed across to the other side, just a few feet ahead of an oncoming car. It is the most devilish thing I've ever seen a squirrel do; I have concluded it must have been a *Horned* Squirrel.

I knew in a flash that Barclay, intent upon the chase, would probably not notice the car, and the car would not have time to brake. "Barclay! Car! Stop!" I yelled, and hoped that he would hear me and, more importantly, that he would obey.

Dogs have the mental ability of a four-year-old human pup, which actually covers a lot of essential life and social skills. But Barclay cannot possibly understand this complicated technological world humans have created. He does well to understand our world of language as well as he does. He knows all about reaction lag time, but does not grasp steel, internal combustion, tonnage, momentum. He does not know the danger he is in. In a world far too complex for him to understand, Barclay needs a master.

As Barclay's master, it is my job to teach him to listen and understand what I tell him. It is my job to provide for his basic creaturely needs – water, food, outside time, exercise, shelter, hygiene and safety. It is my job to keep an eye out ahead, anticipating threats and dangers before they materialize. It is my job to understand the complexities of this world that Barclay can *not* understand.

It is *not* Barclay's job to understand and anticipate all the possible dangers of this world - he can't possible do it; it is Barclay's job simply to listen to the voice of his master.

He did. I called, "Stop!" and practically in mid-stride, Barclay stopped on the spot, balanced on the curbstone.

Humans can't possibly understand the complexities of life. Oh, any eight-year-old can program the newest techno-system with ease. But can you understand your eleven-year-old? Do you know how to talk with a teenager? Can you navigate the rapids of love, the storms of emotion? Can you explain to the elderly when it is time to surrender one's independence... and the car keys? Can your eye penetrate the twilight of death? The economy, geo-political change, let alone the mysteries of the future, or the meaning of life?

In a complex world, humans need a Master. It is the Master's job to provide for your needs, to teach you what you need to know for a productive life, to keep an eye out for all the dangers that lie ahead, to help you recognize and accept your limitations, to understand what you and I can't possibly understand. It is your job simply to listen and heed, even when you're dashing hell-bent after that next squirrel in the road.

2.

MASQUERADE

We arrived at the state park – can't remember where - with mountain lake, wide green swale, picnic grounds, campsites. Lots of families were picnicking that afternoon. So were the geese: *hundreds* of them. Flocks of Canadian geese *everywhere*.

I let Barclay – then an impetuous young Schnauzer, little more than a puppy – romp while I set up the tent. Kept an eye on him, figuring he'd chase geese. He was excited alright... but not by geese: he discovered goose *poop*. Swaths of grass were coated in thick, slimy gray goose poop. Barclay thought he had died and gone to doggy heaven. He frolicked and *rolled* in it.

Barclay's naturally gray, so from a distance he didn't look much different. Close up, he had a full-body pompadour. Even closer, he *stank*. Oh, it was bad. Very, *very* bad. And he was so pleased, as he proudly strutted and displayed his new odor. Then... he leapt into my arms.

Anyone who's had a dog knows they like to roll in nastiness. Why? They like to smell different than they normally do. It makes perfect sense on the hunt: it's easier to stalk your prey if you don't smell like a predator. I guess gazelle don't notice a hungry pack of buffalo dung closing in on them. This isn't so unlike human behavior: just look at all the perfume and aftershave ads that hint at sexual conquest. Cover your scent for the hunt.

However, for dogs it's not just about the hunt – dogs simply love to *stink for the sake of stinking*. They show it off to other dogs, and they compare stench. This, too, makes perfect sense. Human children – of all ages –

like to dress up as ghosts and witches, pirates and cowboys, knights and damsels. We have special holidays around masquerades - like Halloween and Mardi Gras. We have all kinds of costumed festivals like Scottish Highland Games, Renaissance Faires, and Civil War reenactments. Since people are visual, we change the way we *look* to pretend we're somebody else. Why shouldn't dogs like to masquerade, too? Since dogs aren't all that visual, dress them up like Elvis or bumblebees for Halloween and they obviously won't share our enthusiasm. Dogs rely more on their noses, so when *they* dress up and play pretend, they don't change the way they *look;* they change the way they *smell.*

Poor Barclay. I held him under a spigot, and scrubbed. The stuff was oily and the water only rolled off. It took a long time to get him passably clean, and it was clear we couldn't stay there. I packed the car, and we left for other parts. I threw my sweatshirt away. His disguise unappreciated, Barclay was sooo disappointed.

Now, dogs don't want to smell bad all the time. It's a special treat, and they like to parade it. Eventually, it wears off or they clean it up. Masquerading is fun for a while, but not *always.*

People are not so wise. We all like to pretend we're somebody else part of the time, but an awful lot of people pretend they're somebody else all of the time. City kids dress like rodeo cowboys and drive pickup trucks, or good kids emulate prison gangstas and cheap hookers. Middle-aged people disguise their hair color (or lack of hair altogether) and pretend to be young. We inject ourselves with deadly toxins, we endure the cosmetic surgeon's knife, even radical and risky procedures, to permanently change our nose, chin, eyebrows, tummy, breasts, buttocks... Because we hope if only we *look* like somebody else, we might actually *feel* like somebody else.

That's our problem: we don't like who we are down deep inside. No perfume, no hoodie, no sports car, no hair transplant, no injection, no surgery can change who we are. Even God won't change who we are: when he gives us a "new heart," he doesn't turn us into somebody else entirely, rather he helps us to become more authentically *ourselves.*

So you can pretend every now and then, but in the final analysis: Like yourself. Be yourself. Figure out Who-You-Are, and then *be* Who-You-Are. That's who you were made to be, and you can be yourself better than anybody else. When you spend your whole life pretending to be someone you aren't, it's like being dressed up in goose poop. Sooner or later, it's going to stink.

I think Barclay pretty much accepts who he is. He likes to dress up every now and then in other smells, but he's quite content to go back and be himself when the fun is over.

So what have *you* been rolling in?

3.

MOST LOST

It was a Relay for Life, a walkathon to raise money and awareness in the fight against cancer. Dozens of sponsoring organizations set up tents around the perimeter of the walking track to provide cold water or hot coffee for their walkers - some have sandwiches, others cook out – and they compete for best decorations. Some Relays last all day; the one I have in mind was an all-night event. Bands played, crowds cheered, and politicians did, well, whatever it is politicians do. And people walked. Around and around they went, racking up the miles and, with each mile, sponsoring dollars. The only break was for the Survivors' Walk: the track was lined with candles in honor of beloved cancer victims, and the cancer survivors walked, slowly and surrounded by cheering and weeping onlookers, once around the track.

My church youth group was participating, so I went to show my support and help out. I took my Schnauzer Barclay along. Barclay does well off-leash, is extremely well-behaved, even gentlemanly, and has always been a welcome guest. The teenagers made a point to pet and pamper him. Barclay was in doggy heaven.

I signed up to walk in the time slots when others could not come, or regular walkers were trying to catch a meal. I left Barclay in someone's care, and told him to *stay.* Off I went. I didn't get very far, when one of the kids came after me: Barclay had run away. I figured he was looking for me, so I backtracked. The track was *very* crowded and it was slow going.

I'm tall, so I could see where the flow of moving heads was interrupted, like an eddy in the stream of humanity. As I neared, there was Barclay zigging and zagging through the legs. In his eyes was sheer panic – the most frightened I have ever seen him. He was lost among the legs: most lost in the crowd.

There are people who enjoy living in big cities or apartment blocks; they say they like the "anonymity." Meaning nobody knows them, they don't know anybody but whom they choose to know. "Nobody's in my business," they say, which leaves me wondering what business they are in they don't want anyone to know about. They want – or think they want – to be lost in the crowd.

I prefer a small town – enough people to have supermarkets and hardware stores, but not so many as to be anonymous. When people feel anonymous, they can be anonymously *rude* or *cruel.* Why else do you think there is so much cyber-bullying through e-mail, Facebook, and Twitter these days? Face-to-face familiarity breeds a certain minimum of civility. Do people nose around in my business? Undoubtedly. But they also care if they see somebody else nosing around in my bushes when I'm not home. Like Barclay, I want just enough others around me to feel supported, but not so many that I get lost in a faceless stream of humanity.

Humans need friends; we need "verbal reinforcement" and "meaningful touch." We need people who slap us on the back with an encouraging, "You can do this!" We need a hand to hold, a shoulder to cry on, when the stuff of life overwhelms us. We need others to be accountable to, who keep us honest when we want to lie to ourselves. Sometimes you can find the occasional rogue lone wild dog, but dogs really only thrive in a pack; humans need a pack, too. But an anonymous pack...is no pack.

Jesus spent part of his time surrounded by thousands, part of his time alone with God in the wilderness. Most of his time, though, he spent with a small group of disciples and friends. They were in his business, and he was in theirs. But they were forging deep, life-altering bonds that changed the world as we know it.

I wove my way through the crowd to Barclay and called him - had to call a couple of times till he calmed down enough to actually hear me. He leapt into my arms and licked me profusely. This time as I made my way around the track, I carried him. Later, when the crowd had thinned a bit, I walked him on a leash: he preferred it that way, to ensure we weren't separated again.

Being alone is not being lost – that's just solitude. You're only lost if you're surrounded by things that impede your vision, hindering you from getting your bearings and finding your direction. That could be trees...or legs. You are most lost in the crowd, most lonely among faceless strangers in whose eyes you see no bright glint of recognition. So find some friends, or move where you know you can find some. And I think Barclay would add: then never let them out of your sight.

4.

THE RIDE AROUND THE BLOCK

Thinking that my dog Barclay would be bored walking the same old route every day, I decided to take him for an outing. We climbed into the car and drove out into the country. He was curious at first, then gradually lost interest and settled in to nap. Not what I had expected: I thought he would become more and more excited as we moved into new territory with new scenery and scents. When I stopped and took him for a walk, well, he found *that* interesting enough, and maybe that part was a bit of an outing for him. We headed home.

Barclay was napping...until we got a few blocks from the house. Suddenly he sat up, sniffed the air, and hopped up to the window, watching everything very intently. It was the most excitement he had shown all day. He's excited, I thought, because he knows we're almost home. Ahh, the naïve human!

Eventually I discovered it didn't matter if we were coming or going: Barclay was most excited, and most attentive, when we were riding in *familiar territory*. This has proven true not just of Barclay, or only Schnauzers, but all of our dogs, regardless of breed. If you want to give a dog a real thrill, roll down the windows a little, and drive them *very slowly* along the same route where they usually take their walks. Ride them around the block: the thrill of the familiar.

One of my seminary professors, Dr. James Loder, always said: "There is nothing more boring than endless novelty." We students would all nod sagely, but in reality we didn't have a clue what he meant. Young and stupid, we still thought new stuff - new scenery, new clothes, new love - was always the most exciting, and that old, familiar stuff was boring. After all, don't they say, "Familiarity breeds contempt"? How could it be otherwise?

In fact, what we actually find "new" and "exciting" is something familiar...with just a *little something* changed. Creative genius is simply the art of combining familiar elements in fresh and unfamiliar ways. My mother once worked for Opinion Research, evaluating what kinds of cars people might buy. She told us how in 1943 the cars of the 'sixties, 'seventies, and 'eighties were already on the drawing table. But her survey showed nobody wanted any of *those* - not in 1943: they wanted something like the 1942 car with a slightly more aerodynamic grille. The latest fashion is something from two decades ago, just in a different color.

Familiarity takes the uncertainty out of novelty; too much novelty is stressful. I lived in Europe for many years, and if you want to see the world, skip the big tours. Fourteen-Countries-in-Twelve-Days *is* "endless novelty" – my folks tried that one time and found after a couple of days it all ran together into a blur, leaving them physically and emotionally exhausted. All they remembered of their trip was how tiring it was. Well, what would Barclay enjoy? To see Europe, pick one region of one country; stay in one place and take day trips into the countryside. Give it time to *become familiar*, and you'll be able to see and appreciate little details here and there that make it memorable.

What Barclay finds so exciting about *riding* around the block is that he knows this territory - the usual landmarks, the usual smells - but he is seeing (and smelling) it from a new perspective, a slightly different angle, and it all appears a little bit new again. But because it's familiar, he's not intimidated or overwhelmed. He can appreciate the new, because it is nestled in the familiar.

People get suckered into the lure of endless novelty all the time. A man in mid-life crisis abandons his wife and family to hunt for a new place, new job, new girlfriend. Churches fight and split over the familiar, traditional worship style versus a stripped-down, new, contemporary one. We get bored with the familiar, and haven't yet learned how boring endless novelty can be. You'll discover most "Contemporary" churches pretty soon include a lot of old Gospel hymns in their repertoire.

If I'm bored with my house, or my job, or my marriage, or my religion, or whatever, I don't have to jettison everything and invent something radically new in order to re-infuse some excitement into my life. Extreme novelty only brings uncertainty, tension, frustration, intimidation, exhaustion. It is enough if I take a "ride around the block": only change a *little* something, or find a fresh perspective on things – that is, bring just a little something new into the familiar. Suddenly *everything* looks new and different.

And sometimes all that really needs to be a little different is me.

5.

BATH TIME

"Barclay," I call, "Daddy's going to take a bath. Do you want to come take a bath?" I'm trying to sound as matter-of-fact as possible. Schnauzers are not water dogs. I did once get his sons Braxton and Cullen to frolic in a mountain stream – we were supposed to be fly fishing, but you can guess how well the trout were biting when dogs are romping in the stream; we lost interest in fish pretty quick. Barclay, however, true to his Schnauzer credo, avoids water like poison. I call again. With the air of a martyr, Barclay rolls his eyes up at me, filled with both suffering and reproach. Then silently, stealthily, he slinks away into the shadows to hide.

Some of our dogs tolerate bath time better than others, but none of them seem to enjoy it. They certainly don't look forward to it. You would think they would like the cool water on a hot day, the individual attention, the massaging effect of lathering and rinsing, the feeling of clean fur. No.

I'm not sure humans are much better. Don't know about babies, who don't have a lot of say in the matter, but toddlers quickly associate "bath time" and "No!" in their minds *and* vocabulary; in some families it's the biggest power struggle of the day. We have to learn to appreciate a good bath. I didn't enjoy bath time until we moved to a house with a shower – I discovered I *loved* showers, and would pretend I was taking long walks in the rain. Still dislike sitting in a bathtub, though, and I just don't feel clean when I'm done. But there are lots of people – mostly female people, I suspect - who would lounge in a bubble bath till they shrivel into little prunes. Bath time is an acquired taste.

The Romans loved baths – built public bathhouses all over their Empire. In the Dark Ages, baths were feared as something wimpy and unhealthy: makes you wonder if what made the Dark Ages so dark was only a layer of grime.

Practically every religion that has any kind of redemption or forgiveness at its core will have some version of bath imagery. There is a washing, a cleansing of the soul more or less parallel to the washing of the body. Slough off the grime of sin or worldliness or materialism or karma or whatever. Get clean inside.

Early Judaism had washings, especially for the priests, though we don't know much about it except for the existence of ritual baths at the monastery of Qumran (of Dead Sea Scrolls fame). John the Baptist got his nickname from a similar practice in the Jordan River, and Jesus picked it up from him. We're never told how John or Jesus baptized, so evidently the *how* was not that important:

important was *why*. It involved repentance – literally "rethinking" – which meant admitting the bad things we do and then, well, doing things *differently.* Wash the outside, and change the inside.

The image of washing is really very good. We all know that squeaky-clean, tingly feeling when we scrub off layers of sweat and dirt; it's like our skin can breathe again. The idea is to have that tingly feeling *inside*, like you can start over fresh, like you can breathe again. Wash away the layers of guilt, regret, bad habits, selfishness, bitterness, and so forth. Bath time.

But humans, like Schnauzers, do not naturally take to bath time – whether washing the body or the soul. It becomes a power struggle, like there's some huge hurdle to jump, an impassable threshold that we only cross *in extremis.* We excuse, we rationalize, we blame everybody else; we just won't admit and change. Things have to get sooo bad, sooo out of control, that *anything* would have to be better... even (shudder) a *bath*.

Ironic, though, that once you do take that unthinkable step, you feel so much better you wonder why you put it off for so long. I guess it's an acquired taste.

6.

AS BIG AS YOU WANNA BE

I opened the back door to let out the dog. Barclay wasn't a year old, a miniature Schnauzer not even twenty pounds wet. Then I realized my mistake: I hadn't looked first. Sniffing about in my front yard was an enormous Doberman Pincer, who could snap Barclay's neck with one bite.

Barclay saw him, too. Before I could call him back, Barclay took off like a small, silver rocket. And he sounded like one: he wasn't barking, he was emitting a low rumbling growl. He meant business. The Doberman bolted, tucked his tail and ran to the street. Barclay chased him at full speed all the way down the block, then trotted home with satisfied gait and head held high.

That day, I discovered terriers are completely oblivious to differences in size and strength. As far as Barclay was concerned, that Doberman was no larger and no stronger than he was. And the Doberman? He didn't see any difference, either; in his mind, he was just as small and vulnerable as Barclay. Barclay is *as big as he wants to be.*

My dogs fight among themselves every now and then to determine pecking order in the pack. They snarl and snap at each other, butt chests. Then it's over. It doesn't matter which is physically bigger or stronger: it's a contest of determination and courage. The victor simply has the stronger will, the *bigger heart.*

God well knows that the race does not always go to the fastest, nor the prize to the strongest. So he tells a ragamuffin tribal confederation of former slaves and nomads, who can't get along and don't trust their own leaders, to storm into hostile, fortified territory and take it by force. Boy, does God have a ridiculous sense of humor.

In preparation for the invasion, Moses sends in a Long-Range Reconnaissance Patrol to spy out the lay of the land and military strength. But these twelve guys are not military material: picture a bunch of desert bumpkins walking around town gawking slack-jawed in wonder.

A good reconnaissance unit gathers information, but leaves strategy and military feasibility to the field commander. But these guys? Not only is their report useless, they presume to decide feasibility, right out in public. "No way!" ten say, "We can't do it; they're bigger and stronger than we are. The place is full of giants!" After *that*, they're right: there's no way the Hebrews could conquer anything. Demoralized, they don't have the heart for it anymore.

The other two - Caleb and Joshua - you wonder if they were on the same bus tour. They saw the same things, but come away with a *very* different assessment. "Let's go," they call, "we can do this. Piece of cake." They get outvoted ten-to-two, and the stage is set for the Hebrews to return to the wilderness for the next forty years.

The ten would say they're just being realists: we have X number of average-sized attackers, going up against X-Y-Z numbers of giant-sized defenders. We're a ragtag bunch of nomadic raiders going up against disciplined troops and well-defended fortifications. Face facts: it can't be done.

Caleb and Joshua are no less realists than the other ten, but the ten only take into account part of the data. They look at numbers, size, relative military strength. They do NOT take into account the power of determination and faith, the strength of resolve and courage, the intangible qualities of heart and will that allow a little Barclay to chase away a huge Doberman Pincer.

Nor do they reckon with...*God.* Joshua and Caleb do: "If the Lord is pleased with us, he will give it to us! Don't be afraid of the people..." Step out in faith to do what God says to do, then God will see to it that it succeeds.

You can see your Promised Land just over the hill there, but it seems unattainable. Too many high walls, too many fierce giants. That Doberman is just too big. You either surrender to God, or you'll surrender to the giants. With God, you have nothing to fear. The battle is not decided by strength and numbers, but by heart and will, by determination and courage, and by obedient faith.

Giants, Dobermans – it's all the same. Don't tell me you're smaller than little Barclay, because in his eyes and in his heart he's bigger than anything. *It never matters how big the dogs confronting you are, because you are as big as you wanna be.*

7.

"KU-WU-WU"

"Ku-Wu-Wu!" demanded Barclay, as he glanced over his shoulder and cut his eyes at me. He jerked his head, raised one eyebrow, and repeated, "Ku-Wu-Wu." He was clearly saying something, but I couldn't figure out what he wanted. He tried a couple more times, and finally flopped down on the floor with a grunt. He was grumpy. Schnauzers do grumpy well.

I think I was paying the bills – writing checks, balancing the checkbook. Important stuff. I finished folding everything in envelopes, applied stamps, and made ready to take them to the post office. "Barclay," I asked quietly, "you wanna go with Daddy?" His ears perked up. I headed for the door, then paused, glanced over my shoulder at him, jerked my head toward the door with one eyebrow raised, and said, "C'mon!"

Then it hit me, of course. Barclay was doing the exact same thing. Only, since dogs have no real lips, he could not say M's or N's or B's or P's; they would all come out like W's. Try it yourself – talking without using your lips – and you'll see what I mean. "Come on" breaks down to Ku-Mah-N – no "M", no "N" – so Ku-Wu-Wu. Not only did Barclay understand English, he could *speak* it...after a fashion.

If you're going to live in somebody's world, it's good to learn to speak their language. When I first went to Germany, I could say Yes, No, and count to twelve in German. Useless. The first thing I did was teach myself to ask for the restroom... but then I couldn't understand the directions. Sigh. Ordering food, counting money, reading signs, buying necessities: need drove me to learn *quickly*. They tell me I learned the language in record time. All I knew is that I couldn't learn it *quickly enough*.

Over time, I met lots of Americans who would *not* learn the language. Granted, not everyone could: tourists might not have opportunity, or be in the country long enough. Soldiers stationed there had a hard time learning German even if they wanted to, because they spent most of their time on an English-speaking military base: they had little exposure and even less time to practice. I have sympathy for those. But there were always some visitors who had no intention of ever learning a single word of somebody else's language. Ever. Anywhere. Just expected everybody else to kowtow to their needs, to understand *their* language. They forgot whose country they were in.

You don't even have to be in a foreign country to feel like you are. Just discuss momma's estate with a probate lawyer, or investments with a stockbroker, and see how much you understand. Put a high-church

Anglican and a hell-fire Primitive Baptist together: they can talk about the exact same thing, and you wouldn't know it. Two people can both speak English, use the same words, and mean completely different things. So who's going to learn the other's language?

Couples experience this all the time. In his book, *Taste of New Wine*, Keith Miller told how he grew up in a family where the man did yard work and the woman managed the kitchen – including taking out the kitchen trash. His wife's family? Her parents split chores differently, so the woman cooked but the *man* took out the trash. Keith believed it was woman's work, she felt it was man's work, so *no one* would take out the garbage; it was a constant source of arguments and resentments. Until Keith learned that if he wanted to express his love for her in a way she could understand, he had to *speak her language*. He had to take out the kitchen trash, regularly, without being asked or nagged. Ku-Wu-Wu.

If there's somebody you don't get along with, chances are you don't speak the same language. Same words, different meanings. So who's going to learn the other's language? Well, how about you? If you don't make a start of it, it probably won't happen at all...ever...and the miscommunication will only go from bad to worse. If you try, I think you'll discover it's easier than you fear. I mean, if even a dog can learn to speak English, how hard can it be?

8.

THE DOG WHO DOESN'T LIKE MEN

My wife had gone on a working vacation for a few days, and was due to come home when she called. "Dear, there's this dog that I told you about – the old one no one wants. I know we have so many dogs already, but I was thinking we could foster her until we can find another home for her. Can I please bring her home with me? Please?" Her voice was plaintive. "Well," I answered, "I'm kinda an old dog myself, so bring her on." "Thank you," she gushed, "I'll be home in two hours." It was supposed to be a four-hour trip; some quick reckoning told me that meant she was already halfway home... with the dog. "Oh," and she added hurriedly before hanging up, "they tell me she doesn't like men..." Click.

She had been warned Belle did not like men - *really* did not like men - and that might be a problem. Nevertheless my wife decided we would take her in, at least temporarily. As she drove those four hours home, she worried the whole way how the dog would respond to me. Would Belle be aggressive? Would we be able to handle her?

Belle is a large yellow Labrador Retriever - I wonder if she has some Golden Retriever in her genes. We're told she's a little over eight years at this point, but she looks twelve at least. She has had life-threatening health problems, and still requires occasional follow-up. When Ceci got her, Belle had been kept in a small kennel box for months; with almost no exercise, she was seriously overweight and her long claws had begun to curl; she couldn't run more than three or four steps. Her eyes were dull and sad, no, *hopeless.* Everything else we know had to be painstakingly pieced together out of unsubstantiated hints and rumors.

Belle had belonged – we were told – to a woman who got her around her fortieth birthday. Her "momma" had drifted into drugs, finally methamphetamines. She'd go on binges, disappearing for three or four days at a time, leaving Belle shut in without food, sometimes without water. It was a hard life.

We can only surmise how Belle came to dislike men. Her owner had been married once; the ex-husband allegedly dealt drugs and ran with a violent crowd. There seems to have been some unsavory males around. I guess if that's all you knew, you'd dislike men, too.

Belle's owner was murdered in her home at the age of forty-seven, the victim of a drug-vendetta against her ex-husband. Belle was in the house at the time. The killer... was probably a man.

Belle was shunted off onto an overworked dog rescuer who really didn't have the place or time for one more, but couldn't bear to see her put down. For the next eight or nine months, Belle lived in that kennel box. She was let out twice a day to stretch and do her business. Otherwise she lay there...and ate. Her foster parent held out little hope of ever finding a permanent home for her – after all most people want a cute little puppy, not an old, neglected and heartbroken dog with health issues.

And so my wife heard about Belle, and after much prayer and deliberation, found herself driving across the Carolinas with a big yellow Lab, the Dog-Who-Doesn't-Like-Men. That's when she called to ask me. But then, we both understand how precious a safe haven can be. Yeah, bring her on.

But now I had to wonder how Belle would react to me – this Dog-Who-Didn't-Like-Men. She might avoid me, and slink away to hide. Or growl menacingly. Or bite. Would I need to protect myself somehow? Or just take the risk?

Ceci called again just before she arrived, so I could be waiting on the porch. She let Belle out of the car and through the picket gate into the front yard. After sniffing for a few moments, Belle saw me; she wheeled and bolted towards me as fast as she could. Ceci held her breath. I extended the back of my fist for Belle to smell. She paused only a moment, pushed my hand aside, and then... buried her muzzle between my knees. And with a deep sigh, she leaned into me. She was home.

Since that moment, Belle is a Daddy's Girl. The-Dog-Who-Doesn't-Like-Men sits by my chair, lies at my feet, rolls over for tummy rubs, stands with her face leaning against my thigh – all with a funny little contented grin only Labs can make.

Call it a drama of redemption. Like all the People-Who-Don't-Like-God, who hold God responsible for whatever disappointments life has dealt them. Yet He waits on the porch for just the right moment when we finally can come Home. When we meet Him, we know Him, and realize we are safe at last.

It's also a parable of gratitude. After a hard life, Belle knows she's received a second chance; after danger and deprivation, she's safe now. And she appreciates it – her little Lab smile tells me so. Jesus said that whoever has been given much, loves much. Actually, we all have been given much; we all have much to be grateful for. Foolishly, when life is good, we like to think we earned it. It's when life is hard that we recognize grace for what it is.

Belle doesn't overthink things. The Dog-Who-Doesn't-Like-Men knows only she once was lost, but now she's found. And that's enough for her.

9.

ELEPHANTS

Barclay sees shapes. Not all dogs do: many, like his son Braxton, see only movement. If a rabbit sits perfectly still in an open field, Braxton would not see it. He would know that something is there, because he could smell it if the wind is right, but he wouldn't know which way to look. I have held his head aiming straight at a squirrel motionless on the bird feeder just a few feet away, and Braxton would jerk away to watch leaves swaying in the breeze. But not Barclay: he sees and recognizes shapes. *He* sees the still rabbit, the motionless squirrel.

Barclay also loves cows. When he sees them grazing quietly in a rolling field, heads down, he stands at the car window and barks excitedly. Braxton doesn't see anything moving out there, so he looks around with interest, then gives Barclay a puzzled look. He can't figure out what his papa's so excited about. But Barclay sees; he knows.

Another one of Barclay's favorite things is Elephants. No, not the big gray beasts with tusks and trunk – not real elephants. As he gazes across the countryside, he sees here and there herds of great round beasts grazing silently in the field: Hay Bales. They stand there unmoving, heads down, like cows. They probably even smell a little like cows – cows do take on the scent of their fodder. He clearly thinks they're huge animals of some kind, so I call them "Elephants."

I'm not sure what he thinks of them. Is he afraid of them? Or does he want to chase them? Are they friend or foe, prey or predator? I assume, at any rate, he imagines them like great cows. But who can be sure?

People see shapes, like Barclay. We see the rabbit, the squirrel. We can even recognize Aunt Helen from behind. And of course, we see the great Hay Bales and know they are only Hay Bales, nothing more. Only ranchers get excited about Hay Bales.

There are an awful lot of times, though, that we see, but don't recognize. We see the husband with beer for breakfast, but don't recognize the drinking problem. We see the bruises, but can't see the pattern of abuse. Or maybe we see the impossibly wonderful circumstances, but can't recognize the miracle. We see God all over the place, but hardly ever recognize that it's God. As far as we know, it could just be Hay Bales.

And like Barclay, sometimes we see things, but we don't know what they mean. Is it a predator, something we need to run from, or is it prey, something we ought to pursue? Is it just another Hay Bale? Or is it really an Elephant?

Our vision is especially bad when we gaze into the distant Future. The land of the Future is quite foggy, the terrain unfamiliar. There we see shapes, great looming shadows that appear to be rushing toward us. Of course they are not rushing toward us, that's just an illusion created by the turning of Earth; they are probably grazing motionless, heads down. We, like Barclay, get quite excited – sometimes with anticipation, more often with dread. It could be Elephants...or maybe just Hay Bales. We can't tell from this distance, or from this angle. And we expend an awful lot of energy barking, growling, snarling, hiding, or whatever, because we think we maybe see shapes looming on down the road.

As we all know, most of the eventualities we fear never actually materialize. The lump turns out to be only a cyst; the verge of bankruptcy becomes a payment plan. The future we get excited about? That doesn't always materialize either: most lottery tickets do not win.

As a general rule, the future holds more of what the present contains, and if it's going to be any different, it's because we decide to make it different – for better or worse or just different. Odds are those shapes looming on the horizon of my history will be Hay Bales, not Elephants. What you make of the shapes around you, and ahead of you, is up to you.

10.

UNFLAPPABLE
Barclay and the Goose

A flock of geese were feeding in the distance on the broad grassy field. I parked the car, and let out my two Schnauzers to stretch and do...well...what dogs do best.

Suddenly, a large gander charged across the field toward the dogs, flapping his wings menacingly and honking loudly. A goose attack is serious business – one blow from those wings can break bones. He first went after Braxton, who was little more than a puppy at the time. Fortunately, Braxton was quick enough to evade the attack, run one circle around the gander, and come yapping back to the car for refuge as fast as his little legs could carry him.

Barclay stood still and watched this quietly. As the goose turned and charged at him, Barclay did not bark. He did not *move*.

Barely a foot away, the goose stopped – beak outstretched, wings spread. They stood there facing one another for several seconds... *long* seconds. Then, almost in slow motion, Barclay tipped his head to one side, then the other.

The goose - visibly nonplussed - settled back, folded his wings, then slowly tipped *his* head to one side, then the other. *Very* slowly both of them leaned forward, sniffed, touched noses, and then settled back. Barclay tipped his head to one side, then the other. The goose responded by tipping his head one way, then the other.

Respectfully, Barclay stepped forward, buried his nose in the goose's chest feathers and sniffed deeply as the goose peered down at him. Barclay stepped back, tipped his head one way, then the other. The goose tipped his head as well, this way, then that way. Satisfied, Barclay turned and calmly trotted back to the car. The goose flapped once and honked farewell. True story.

People fight about the silliest things. Any petty grievance gets turned into a titanic clash of wills and personalities. One unhappy person says something needlessly snippy or snide, the other responds in annoyance or anger, and soon it escalates into a war of words and wills; still other people get dragged into the mudslinging and are pressured to choose up sides. You'd think Christians would be immune to this – after all, we all *know* we should relinquish our selfish wills and forgive as generously as Christ has forgiven us – but church people are among the snippiest people, and church fights are among the most brutal there are.

According to Barclay, *if you remain unflappable, then it can't escalate into a flap.* It's Biblical: "Those who are hot-tempered stir up strife, but those who are slow to anger calm contention" *(Proverbs 15.16)*. Anger can be contagious, but so can calmness. If someone attacks you, don't attack them back, and pretty soon everything settles back down. Life has enough challenges without creating unnecessary turmoil.

You know, when you refuse to be drawn into a big flap, you sometimes find new friends in the most unlikely places. At least, that's how it looks to Barclay. And he should know.

11.

CHRISTMAS AMBUSH

For Christmas, Ceci's dogs Munch and Maude would get a toy, just the thing for her energetic Lab-Doberman brother and sister. It was called a "weasel" – a battery powered ball with a furry "tail" that would scoot around the room erratically. She wrapped it carefully, and as she placed it under the tree, she pointed it out to them: "This is for you," she said.

Christmas Eve around three in the morning, Ceci was awakened by a racket in the living room. She rushed in... to find Munch and Maude barking and leaping around excitedly. And zigzagging across the room was the weasel.

The two dogs had sneaked down in the middle of the night, picked out *their* one present – nothing else was disturbed - carefully unwrapped it, and as they took turns chewing on it, somehow managed to turn on the switch. Santa had been here, let the play begin!

Even as kids, we learn to unwrap our presents... Shoot, most three-year-olds will unwrap everybody else's presents, too, if given half a chance. But as adults, I guess, we forget how to do it. Maybe we've gotten used to leaving it to the kids or grandkids to unwrap gifts for us.

I'm talking, of course, about the gifts of God. Starting with Jesus... but extending to the gift of the Holy Spirit, the various other gifts of the Spirit, all those promises just waiting to be claimed. I don't know how many church people I've known through the years who said that, yes, they'd been given much through Jesus... but they never bothered to unwrap it and put it to use in their lives.

So what has God given you for Christmas...and Easter...and Pentecost, that you haven't unwrapped yet? Munch and Maude couldn't wait. So what are *you* waiting for?

12.

YOUR MARK

Dogs are always leaving their mark. You wonder how their bladders could ever hold that much, but then, each time they leave a mark it's only a few drops. Just enough to leave a smell that says: "I was here."

My dogs leave their mark in other ways. Sometimes they will start pawing and scratching the ground as they make little growls – all very assertively. No, they are not covering their waste, but *accentuating* it. Little sweat glands in their paws secrete musk into the soil: it is the most aggressive form of territorial marking, indicating to other dogs that *"this* is *my* turf, and I am prepared to defend it."

Some marks are unconscious. For many years, until he grew too old and arthritic to leap up onto and down from the furniture, Barclay would sleep on my bed. On chilly nights, he would stare at me until I awoke, then poke me with his nose till I let him under the covers to warm up. So one morning in late spring I found myself scratching my stomach – a lot. I hitched up my shirt and found the telltale dark pink, blistery signs of poison ivy: five spots, specifically, a lozenge-shaped one and, aligned in an arc along one side, four perfectly round dots. A perfect Barclay-sized, itchy pawprint on my tummy. His mark.

We humans are always leaving our mark. Sometimes we do it intentionally: we reorganize the company, write a book, get elected to public office, discover something, plant a tree. Anything to leave a more or less lasting mark on the landscape, or history, or humanity. It's our legacy, something to be remembered by.

Yet we leave unintentional marks as well. An unthinking, careless word of criticism or anger; a kind deed that we do without expecting anything in return; a few extra moments spent with a lonely soul; a few unwise moments behind the wheel on the way home from the party. Good and bad, knowingly and unknowingly, we leave marks on the lives of others that can last for a long time to come. Our own little poison-ivy pawprints.

I am a professional Interim Pastor: it's my job to come into churches after the pastor leaves, and get them ready for a new one. I come and go a lot. When I arrive, I can see the telltale pawprints of whomever was there before me. And when it's time to leave, I try to take stock of the marks I have left. Some I might be aware of. There are a number of goals I usually have to accomplish: calming a shell-shocked congregation; adjusting staff and budget to an appropriate and affordable size; stabilizing financial giving; managing personnel turnover; decentralizing decision-making to the board members and their committees. But there are also marks I did not know I was leaving behind – some good, some bad. I'd list some of them, but since I didn't know I was leaving them, I can't. I may never know them all, until the clarity of Heaven brings all things to light. And if it itches... I apologize.

The challenge for each of us it to live, speak, and act *consciously* and *intentionally* - at least, as much as we are humanly able. To be able to say, "I was here," and be pleased with all that you accomplished, even in the little, unknowing moments. And do what you can to mitigate those unintentional pawprints you leave on the lives of others, you know, the ones that itch or blister. We owe it to ourselves; we owe it to our friends. One of the things Barclay taught me.

13.

INTERPRETER

For a while I took my Schnauzers, papa Barclay and son Braxton, to work every day. They stayed close to me, and dutifully barked whenever anyone entered the building – useful in a church where back doors often get left unlocked. The church secretary appreciated my furry "burglar alarms."

One day, when I went to lunch it was too hot outside to keep them in the car, so I left "the boys" in my office. While I was gone, someone rang the doorbell...and the dogs went crazy. YAP, YAP, YAP, YAP, YAP! My secretary couldn't hear a thing above their barking. She tried to no avail to hear the other person on the intercom, then at the door, to no avail. YAP, YAP, YAP, YAP, YAP!

I had mentioned that Barclay understood English, but she had always assumed that was simply empty talk, a dog-owner's Daddy-Pride. At her wit's end, she figured this was the occasion to put it to the test. Slowly and firmly she called, "Barclay, it's alright! You can stop barking now!" To her amazement, immediately Barclay fell quiet. But Braxton – well, she hadn't addressed her remarks to *him.* YAP, YAP, YAP, YAP, YAP!

If Barclay understands English - she thought to herself - maybe Braxton does, too. She called, "Braxton, it's alright! You can stop barking now!" But Braxton did *not* know English: YAP, YAP, YAP, YAP, YAP!

On a whim, my secretary tried something else. "Barclay," she called through the door, "tell Braxton it's alright; he can stop barking now." Barclay let out one deep, authoritative *WOOF,* and Braxton fell silent.

Sometimes you need an interpreter, someone who understands both languages and can be a go-between. I worked as an interpreter for a while myself. I translated theological and medical articles for publication, and did consecutive (line-by-line) interpreting for American military chaplains in Germany. Also did a stint as a simultaneous interpreter – the guy behind the curtain with headphones and microphone, listening to one language while he talks in another. Thankfully, I do not have to make a living at it, and the world is a safer place for it.

Funny thing, though, how two people can both speak English and *still* not understand each other. They can use the same words and phrases, and mean completely different things. So they talk and talk, but never really communicate; they get frustrated and talk even more...and *louder.* YAP, YAP, YAP, YAP, YAP! Eventually, they stop talking altogether. That's how marriages, friendships, and international diplomacy fall apart.

Sometimes we need an interpreter, somebody who can help us find a common language. Now, an interpreter is *not* a messenger: you don't send a go-between to talk for you, so you can avoid talking and understanding altogether. *You* have to sit down with the other person and talk, back and forth; the interpreter only helps *clarify* what each one really means. Whether you both can find common ground, well, that's up to you.

Jesus once said that if you and your neighbor don't get along, go talk with him or her one-on-one; if you can't reach an understanding, then take one or two other people with you and try again. Some people think he meant take along somebody to you have a *witness* who can then attest that you really tried to patch up the relationship but that the *other* person was irreconcilable: Bad dog! But I think maybe he meant: find an interpreter, a go-between, who can help you speak the same language. *WOOF!*

14.

UNSEEN WORLDS

Barclay stands riveted to the spot, his nose buried in a clump of grass as he sniffs, snorts, sniffs...*deeply*. He will not leave though I call him, urge him.

Terrier Gracie pauses, one front paw slightly raised, her ears and curled tail erect. Her eyes are glassy, unseeing, as she raises her nose into the breeze. Her nostrils twitch.

Dogs rely on their noses like humans rely on their eyesight. Dogs can see, many see *well*, and are not entirely colorblind as a lot of naïve humans suppose. However, they generally do not assign it the same value that we do. If they go blind with age, they can adapt as long as they can still smell: Barclay has crystallization of the retina, a degenerative eye condition common to ancient Schnauzers, which I imagine is like looking at the world through a prism, but it doesn't seem to bother him as he continues to sniff deeply into his clump of grass.

We are "differently-abled" – I think that's the term these days. Human noses have by a rough count about five million olfactory nerve endings on a membrane about the size of a postage stamp, and we process what we smell in a brain center little bigger than the head of a pin. Dogs, however, have over *two-hundred-twenty million* olfactory nerve endings on an accordion-folded membrane about as big as the dog's entire skin, and they process their smells in a brain center forty times bigger than ours. They can identify smells as faint as one part to one million parts air, some smells even down to one to ten million parts. Which means dogs' noses are *one-hundred-million times more sensitive than ours.*

Actually, dogs have two separate smell organs. The first is the usual one up in the nose, like ours. But they have a second one above the roof of their mouths, the vomeronasal organ, built completely differently - that's the one boy dogs use especially to find girl dogs in heat. Just like two eyes allow us to see in three dimensions, having two smell organs kinda means dogs can *smell in 3-D*.

But what could Barclay possibly discover as he sniffs so long and deeply? I assume he is smelling the mark from some animal, and naturally he will know whether it was a raccoon, possum, or a dog; if dog, then at the very least he can tell its sex, its age, its recent diet, the state of its health, its mood at the time, maybe its breed, and how long ago it was here; if a female dog, he will know if she is in heat, pregnant, or recently had pups, and if she is in the company of other males. Call it an "e-piss-tle" – apologies for the pun – and Barclay is reading and memorizing it word for word.

We humans place an ultimate value on our eyesight: the world we *see* is the world that is. Or so we assume. We want to believe only what we can see. You've heard someone say, "Seeing is believing," or "I'll believe that when I see it." Might have said it yourself. But what if there is a whole other world that can't be seen at all, only smelled?

Modern Science Fiction writers have often speculated about overlapping universes: how many worlds could all exist in the exact same place, but in different dimensions so they are unaware of each other. In a way, they do. Barclay reminds us there is the seen world, and an unseen world – the world that can only be known by scent. And of course, even the seen world only encompasses a limited spectrum of light; there is a whole other dimension apprehended only through non-visible light.

Medieval theologians used to argue over how many angels could dance on the head of a pin. We make fun of them now for discussing in all seriousness something that seems to us so petty and almost childish. But only because we do not understand what they were pondering, namely, whether spirit, and spirit beings, have mass and take up space within this earthly dimension. When they concluded that one pinpoint could simultaneously host an infinite number of angels, they were pretty much saying the same thing as our contemporary Science Fiction authors. All space and time are relative, and unseen dimensions can overlap *infinitely*. Pretty heady stuff.

Overlapping this world is one more world, invisible to the eye, unappreciated even by the nose, known only by the spirit. To limit reality to only what can be seen is naïve – every dog nose testifies to another reality that can only be smelled. There is a reality more real than anything that can be seen. To "see" it you, of course, must first cultivate your sixth, *spiritual* sense. Develop it, train it, practice it... *deeply*. What you will discover is another universe with different laws of physics, where what is otherwise impossible is suddenly possible; what is valuable elsewhere is suddenly worthless. It is "what no eye has seen, nor ear heard: what God has prepared for those who love Him" - and, we might add, what no nose has smelled. Sorry, Barclay.

15.

LETTING GO

I picked out Barclay in 1997 for my first wife. She could be very skilled at training dogs, and took almost child-like delight in playing tug of war, chase, and hide-and-seek with him. Barclay clearly thought of *me* as his master, though; he was a Daddy's Boy. He had fun playing with her, but I always suspected he felt safer with me. Once my wife was jumping up and down to reach into a high cabinet; Barclay, too young to know better, jumped up and down with her, till he got too wound up and bit her in the back of the leg. She hit him – hard – then tried to kick him. She went ballistic, and screamed for me to hold him so she could kick him some more; I held him all right, but leaned over him and shielded him, catching the blows. I took a pretty good pummeling.

When Barclay turned four, my wife and I went separate ways, and we had to divide up the household. I observed that the more I wanted this or that, the more she wanted it, too; if I showed no especial interest in it, she ceded it willingly. A lot of divorcing couples experience the same kind of power struggle: I suppose it's just human nature. Fortunately, we did not have children to fight over. But who gets the dog? I guessed that if I said I wanted him, she would fight tooth and nail to keep him. Could I trust her with him? Would he be safe? I wrestled with it a long time. So what do you do? *I let go.* "Well," I said at last, "we originally got Barclay for you, so why don't you keep him?" I prayed under my breath, committed him to God's care and protection, and let my wife take him.

The most important things in life must be held lightly, gently, reverently. You have to be willing to let them go. Children: you give them structure, routine, basic rules for safety and more-or-less harmonious coexistence, but they need room to experiment, make their own mistakes and learn their own lessons. In time, they want and need to be their own persons; eventually, if you did your job right, they leave the nest. If you hold them too tightly - control them, mold them too intentionally and too closely in your own image, or use them to live out your own dreams vicariously - they will be stifled and will rebel. Love them and let them go. One day they'll be gone, and that's the way it should be.

Love? Grip someone too tightly, they feel smothered and will pull away - they just need room to breathe. The more you run after them, the further you'll drive them away. But that doesn't just alienate others, it hurts *you*, too. Shakespeare wrote a play about a king who was desperately fearful he would lose the love of his beautiful wife; the more tightly he clung to her, the more anxious he became until at last he had her in a deathgrip, literally, as Othello strangled Desdemona, the love of his life.

Jesus said that everything about God is paradoxical. The way up leads down, the way down leads up. The proud are brought down, the humble lifted up. The rich are pitiable, the poor are blessed. What's whispered in the back room should be announced from the housetop. To rule, be the servant of all. Gain everything by giving everything away. Try to keep your life and you'll lose it; lose it for Jesus, and you'll get it back again. Try desperately to live, and you will die; lay down your life and die, and you will live forever. If it's important, let it go.

I let Barclay go. About six weeks later my wife called. We needed to go over some financial things, like dividing up the taxes. Did I want some of the things she had kept? All the stuff was getting underfoot. And oh, she was dating a guy who was still grieving over his last dog, and wasn't ready to accept a new one. Could I come and get Barclay?

When I picked him up, she shrugged, "It's just as well. He won't play or go outside; all he does is lie under the bed and wait for you to come by. I guess he's just a Daddy's Boy."

I let him go...and he was given back to me. And he's been with me ever since.

16.

SPOILS OF THE HUNT

Whatever it was that Cullen found had to be mighty interesting...

When I walk the Schnauzers, sometimes I'll let one off leash to chase squirrels or other critters. Late one night, I let young Cullen run free to chase some rabbits. He took off; the rabbits scattered. Cullen suddenly stopped in the church parking lot, ignoring the rabbits, to sniff and paw at the asphalt. I called several times, but he didn't come.

I went after him, ready to discipline him for not obeying. He looked up at me, then back down, again up, then down: he wanted me to come see what he had found. What could be so important, more important to a dog than rabbits and squirrels? There between his front paws lay... a *one dollar bill.*

The Psalmist said that God owns "the cattle on a thousand hills." So money is not important to God, except in so far as it is important to *us.* Once a rich man asked Jesus how to be saved...and Jesus told him to give away all his wealth. He went away sad, because his money was more important to him than God or Jesus or eternity or anything else. But then, all who put their faith in money or other possessions will live very sad lives.

In this story, Jesus put his finger on a key truth: *our attitude toward money is a barometer of our spiritual condition.* It reveals our priorities. And God cares *a lot* about our priorities.

God wants to be our number one priority. When we put Him first, everything else will have its fair place. As we yield ourselves and what we own to Jesus for His service, He will make sure we have what we need to live.

God wants other people to be our number two priority - still above money and possessions. So if someone is hungry, I'm supposed to feed him; homeless, I help her find a place to live. This doesn't mean I expect the government to do everything for everybody and simply take all my money to pay for it. No, this is something *I* do, *you* do. Compassion delegated to anonymous institutions - that's not compassion. What concerns Jesus is *our* compassion, *our* priorities.

In the church, we have domesticated Jesus' radical truth into "Stewardship Season." It even sounds dull. Usually around late October or November, we fill out little pledge cards to give the church treasurer an idea how much we plan to contribute next year, then turn them in on "Covenant Sunday." Yawn. From God's perspective, this is my chance to put my money where my mouth is: I *say* I want to live the Jesus way, *say* I put God first, but is it really true? This is where the rubber meets the road – exciting, *dramatic* stuff. It's a pity we've made it so ho-hum.

Ultimately, of course, every dollar I have or ever will have is little more than a gift from somebody else, an unexpected find, like Cullen's dollar. It's not actually mine, but has been entrusted to me only long enough to see what I'm going to do with it. In a way, Stewardship Season really culminates not in "Covenant Sunday," but a couple of weeks later, in *Thanksgiving.*

Cullen's dollar still hangs on the door of the refrigerator, a reminder that what we own is little more than a surprising find, a fortuitous gift. It's all grace. I think Cullen would agree.

17.

BOOMERS

The sky is dark, the air heavy, the wind is picking up. Suddenly there is a flash, and a crash that rolls across the heavens. A Boomer. Our big yellow Lab, Belle, jerks, whines, leans hard against my leg and buries her head in the bend of my knee. She is trembling.

Some dogs are afraid of storms, some are not. Old Maude used to run and hide in a tight, dark place when the barometric pressure dropped and her ears picked up distant thunder. Now it's Belle who comes for reassurance and solace when a storm brews. Our black-and-tan terrier, Gracie, gets antsy in bad weather, though she only watches, alert and cautious, from her bed. Barclay and the other Schnauzers, however, merely glance up

curiously for a second from their beds –
"What was that noise? Oh, just a Boomer..." -
then settle back down for a nap: they sleep
hard when it storms.

When Barclay was a young pup, he wasn't
sure how to respond to thunder. At first he
would be unsettled, when he could hear the
rumble far off, long before I could hear it.
As it neared, he would come looking for me.
When at last there was a thunderclap close
by, he would watch me, to see if he should be
frightened. Now, I grew up in central Florida,
where we used to have fierce summer
thunderstorms every afternoon so regularly
you could set your watch by it. I respect
storms – you won't find me out in the open like
a human lightning rod – but I do not fear
them. It's just Boomers. When he saw I was
not afraid, Barclay wasn't afraid either. And
he taught his sons Braxton and Cullen not to
be afraid.

My wife is uncomfortable when it
storms, though; she jumps when it thunders.

Her dogs watched her and concluded thunder *was* something to fear. Maude hid, Gracie is guarded. Belle – well, she's a new addition to the pack, an older rescue dog from a sad home. I guarantee you, though, her owner had to have been scared of storms: that's where Belle learned to be afraid.

Here is a rule of life we can learn from Barclay and his boys: *when it thunders, look to your Master.* Children watch their parents to see how to react... but who should their parents look to?

Paraphrasing the Bible, God rides the storm like a skateboard. Okay, it's a very *loose* paraphrase. At least, I always thought thunder sounded a little like the rumble and rattle of roller skate wheels. God is not afraid of much of anything, and since he *makes* those lightning bolts, he certainly isn't scared of *them.* So unless you are holding a rod of metal upright over your head in the middle of a naked golf course, or standing out like a sore thumb on top of a bare mountain ridge or boat dock, you probably don't need to be all too afraid either. It's just Boomers.

Life has its storms, its roar and turmoil. We can tremble and hide, run in circles and whine, bury our heads in the laundry... or rest in calm assurance that everything will be alright. It's just another one of those storms. The difference is: where do you look when the thunder crashes?

The Psalmist said: "You keep him in perfect peace whose mind is staid on you, because he trusts in you." When you go through storms, when you face cancer or heart disease, when the country goes through economic turmoil, when your church is beset with uncertainty and worries, *look to your Master.* He isn't scared, and you'll find you're not all that scared anymore either. You can be curious, of course, but you can rest calmly. *It's only Boomers.* Belle is learning all about it now, and she'll be glad to tell you...

18.

OLD FOOL

We have a new dog in the house. A dog rescuer was unexpectedly laid off from work and had to find new homes for her charges: we were given Cheyenne, a two-year old, female white Labrador Retriever. My wife was thrilled – since the passing of Munch and Maude, she has missed the distinctive companionship of large Labs. Would the rest of our pack be thrilled, too?

Cheyenne was well received. But we've been having problems with my old Schnauzer, Barclay. No, he isn't jealous: rather, he has decided she is the most lovely creature he has ever seen, and is utterly smitten. At this point, Barclay is well over thirteen years, that is, ninety-one in dog years; he should be past the whole hormone thing, and none of the plumbing should be working by now, right? Surprise. He would not leave her alone, but day and night would constantly, *constantly* try to display his affection, doggy-style. She was not interested, but was too gentle and submissive to put him in his place; she would shake him off and move, but he trotted after her whimpering passionately. After two weeks, she finally grew so annoyed she growled and snapped at him, but in his gyrations old Barclay had already thrown out his back. For the moment he have peace.

They say there's no fool like an old fool. With time the body may grow old but the passions stay young. Poor Barclay.

I can't fault Barclay. He takes after his master. I married late, and through the years have myself suffered through many, *many* one-sided romances with women who did not want to return my advances but were either too polite or too needy to tell me so. They'd string me along, and I would let myself be strung along, until I ended up frustrated, disappointed, and heartbroken. I kept thinking I'd grow out of it – this penchant for one-sided passion – but alas, it does not dim with age or wisdom. The young fool only becomes an old fool. I will be forever grateful to my wife Ceci for offering me a stable, healthy alternative, or else I'd be out there getting my heart broken once again.

Somehow, I think God has a soft spot in his heart for old fools and unrequited love. He understands...perfectly. The prophets often described Israel like a lost waif whom God took in and raised to young womanhood, then pledged his troth to her. But she? Ignored him, rebuffed him, fooled around with any god and country who would give her the time of day. A real slut. Heartbroken, God would keep swearing he'd had it with her, that he would cut her off for good, but then his passion, or compassion, would get the better of him and he would again try to woo her. Sent her love letters wrapped up in people called "prophets." Wrote poems to her.

Eventually came himself in person to win and claim his bride. That ended badly.

Ahh, the power of God's passion! To endure the self-denigration of Incarnation, every humiliation, even death, for the sake of unrequited love! That's what we celebrate at Christmastime: not just the birth of a baby, but God's most desperate attempt to win the heart of his bride. St. Paul called the Gospel foolishness, but that somehow the foolishness of God is even wiser than the wisdom of men. The majestic glory of the Old Fool.

By the way, the Bride he wants to woo – that's you and me. An awful lot of us creatures are not interested, no thank you, but are too polite or needy to say so. Others of us are too proud and insecure to say yes. So this year, don't string God along any longer: tell him yes or no. Just remember though: you'll never find anybody who will love you more than he does. Not even Barclay.

19.

BRINGING UP THE REAR

Barclay, my old Schnauzer, threw out his back. Something to do with making unwanted advances toward a young female Retriever. Probably served him right, but it pinched the nerve and left his back legs completely paralyzed. Recovery – if he recovered at all - would be long and slow.

Guys, there's probably a lesson for all of us there somewhere. Just saying.

Dogs *have* to walk – it keeps their lungs clear and their digestion working. With ropes, rings, hooks, and rivets I created a harness for his hips. He could walk with his front legs, and I would carry his hind legs just high enough above the sidewalk he wouldn't scrape his feet. I walked him three or four times a day. He would follow his nose, and I would tag along behind.   I call it – quite literally – "Bringing Up the Rear."

I have experience with this kind of thing.   Our old Doberman/Lab Munch lost much of his hindquarter coordination for the last year-and-a-half of his life. He could still walk, but I had to haul his 120 lb. rump up the stairs every night, down every morning. His sister Maude had a spinal lesion that left her largely unable to walk for the last four months of her life, so I carried her out and in, out and in, five times or more every day; I'd stand with her at 3:00 a.m. in the snow. When she died of other causes, she had started to move her legs again. I'm used to Bringing Up the Rear.

The rear – it's the least attractive part of the dog... or the human. Most of the weight's back there, where the big bones are. Add in bladder infections, other digestive issues, and old-dog-incontinence, and it might be smelly, or even messy. It can be hard, nasty work, Bringing Up the Rear.

But it's what love does. You love this creature, or person, enough to bear the burdens they can't bear themselves. Anyone who's ever cared for an invalid understands how compassion stretches your tolerance, just like parents get used to changing diapers.

It is true for human society, every charitable organization, and for the church. In some way, everybody is an invalid. We each have some handicap: some burden we can't carry alone, some blind eye, some embarrassing and messy trait. As we get to know someone on the deeper levels of our humanity, sooner or later we discover the dread secret, the soft underbelly, the distasteful truth, the secret fear: we discover The Rear. And they discover ours. Then the question is: what do we do about it? Throw up our hands in disappointment or anger, hold our nose and get away?

Love Brings Up the Rear. I accept you with all your flaws and failings, your weaknesses and handicaps. What you can't bear alone, I bear with you. Especially the less presentable parts.

After a few weeks, Barclay started moving his feet, then his legs. Over three months later, he can walk now, slowly, though his gait is still quite lumpy. Some days, he can even wag his tail. He may never make a full recovery, but he can stand on his own four feet; he can walk by himself. He just needed some help and some time to heal.

The apostle Paul said: Bear one another's burdens. Sometimes, they themselves are the burden, and they will never heal without help. Love will bear them anyway; it will Bring Up the Rear. You usually don't have to do it forever, just through the most critical phase. Pretty soon they'll start standing on their own feet again. And you'll stand taller, too.

20.

THE OTHER SIDE OF THE HEDGE

Since Ceci and I married, we have six dogs. At first, I would walk them all together: trying to control over three hundred pounds of canine as I manage six leashes. Finally gave up and took them in two shifts. I would take the more rambunctious, smaller dogs around the block, then would walk the *big* dogs together. Brother Munch and sister Maude were large but old, slow, and easy-going. Munch had excellent eyesight, but a so-so nose. Maude, I think, was gradually going blind, but her nose was especially keen.

Our daily route took us along a low rock wall topped by a tall – probably eight feet or more – hedge. Buried somewhere in the hedge was a chain link fence, but the leaves were so dense you couldn't even see it.   The dogs would plod along, stop to sniff; plod on, stop to sniff.

As we sniffed and plodded our way along the wall one evening, Maude suddenly froze, nose twitching, turned her head this way and that, and then faced the hedge. She lowered her head, hair bristling on the back of her neck, and growled softly. I squinted into the leaves; there was nothing to see.   No movement, no sound. But Maude's excellent sense of smell told her what I could not know: there was something or someone on the *other side of the hedge*.

The eyes do not tell us everything about our world. There are things we cannot see or touch, that are nevertheless very real and present.   You recognize them through the other senses – maybe smell, taste, sound. Or maybe *different* senses: a sixth sense...or seventh. We have senses we don't even know we have – they are unconscious, and we do not cultivate them. But there are things we perceive, things we *know*, and we aren't always sure *how* we know them, but we are absolutely certain. When people say, "I'll believe it when I see it," they are being neither realistic, nor skeptical: they are being naïve. Much of what matters in this life is not and never will be visible: it lies on the Other Side Of The Hedge.

Death is one of those hedges that define the boundaries of life. The eyes, ears, hands do not tell us what, if anything, lies on the other side. Most of the time we simply plod and sniff along our path; the hedge is there, we take it for granted, even ignore it, and devote our attention to things closer at hand. But every now and then, something rivets our attention on the hedge itself, and what may be beyond. Often it's a crisis, loss, or tragedy: then we squint into the impenetrable leaves, bristle and growl softly.

At Easter, Christians celebrate the One who actually went to the Other Side Of The Hedge and came back: Jesus has been there. He did not return in order to give us a detailed description of what death and afterlife are like. It is what it is, and we probably don't really have the words to describe it anyway. But he did go and come back to remove the "sting" of death, to take the terror out of it. Because whatever death might bring, he has assured us that HE will be there waiting for us.

The next time you find yourself riveted to the hedge, tense and softly growling: yes, there is something just on the other side. Or rather, Someone. It takes a different, maybe sixth sense to recognize Him. We call it "faith," but I think it's really just an intuitive kind of seeing what you can't see, of grasping what you can't touch, just as real as the usual five senses. The human spirit's intangible sense of smell. Just sniff and you'll recognize Him, always walking right beside you and waiting for you barely an arm's reach away, there on the Other Side Of The Hedge.

118